Quiet Time

Within the depths of
His darkest clouds
God often seems to bury His
richest treasures -
silver streaks of growth,
sterling faith,
precious, gleaming truths -
for His children.

Has a dense
doubt,
pain,
loss,
trouble,
frustrat...
lonelin...

settled over you, dear one?
Search out the treasures of darkness!
The riches of your Heavenly Father hide there -
with your name engraved in silver!
growing in closeness to God.

FROM 'A SILVER PEN FOR CLOUDY DAYS'
BY SUSAN L. LENZKES, ZONDERVAN PUBLISHERS
COPYRIGHT© 1986

"... He causes his sun to rise on
the evil and the good, and
sends rain on the righteous
and the unrighteous."

MATTHEW 5:45

THE TAPESTRY OF LIFE

Christians are not exempt from the natural laws that govern the universe. We may through grace be able to overcome them, but we are not able to avoid them.

There are many dark threads woven into the tapestry of life, and it is our attitude to those dark threads that makes all the difference. God loves us with a perfect love, and He will only weave the dark threads if He can turn them to good effect.

"For this is the Eternal's promise: 'Those who survive the sword shall find grace in the dungeon.'"

JEREMIAH 31:2 (MOFFAT)

GRACE IN THE DUNGEON

You may be caught up in difficult and perplexing circumstances and feel that there is no way out – you are imprisoned and feel you are unable to find a way out of a dungeon of despair.

If you are not able to get out of the dungeon, then God can help you to get the dungeon out of you – to find grace in even the most trying circumstances of life.

*"My grace is sufficient
for you ..."*

2 CORINTHIANS 12:9

A CONSTANT FLOW

When our souls are open to the grace that continually flows towards us from heaven, then every limitation, every difficult situation, every perplexing circumstance can be the setting for a new discovery of God and a new revelation of His love.

Take hold of this truth and make it a reality in your life, that when your circumstances become a dungeon, you can find grace there, not only for yourself, but also enough to pass on to others.

❖

The Lord Jesus Christ is the embodiment of grace. He will never fail to make His way to you, whatever your circumstances and whatever your need. Breathe the calm and peace of His presence into your being and allow God to wrap Himself around you.

There is nothing that God allows to come against you which cannot be used to contribute to a deepening of your character and which cannot be turned into something better.

❖

"For the grace of God that brings salvation has appeared to all men."

TITUS 2:11